MY CURLY LOCKS

ALISHA AIYER

To all the beautiful children who are born with curly hair and dark skin

Contents

Acknowledgements

I would like to thank those who have inspired me to write this book through their judgmental comments, bullying, appreciations and encouragements.
I would also like to thank my parents for encouraging me in writing this book.

About Author

Alisha is a 9 year old girl who loves writing contents, painting, sketching. She also loves to interact with people and strike effective and instantaneous conversation effortlessly even with strangers.

She loves to sing mostly western songs though her favourite singers are Kishore Kumar & Lata Mangeshkar.

ALISHA

My Curly Locks

75th
INDEPENDENCE DAY
2022/8/15 17:16

As you may be wondering, what this story is all about. My name is Alisha Aiyer, and this is my story. I am 9 years old. I was born and brought up in Mumbai. I was born in the hospital called Bhakti Vedanta Hospital. I was the biggest baby in the hospital (that's what my parents say). My mom wished for a girl. My grandma said it's a girl and some stupid people said it's a boy. If you were there and you thought it was going to be a boy, here's something I bought for you.

Dear person,

I would like to congratulate you for being 100% stupid.

Here I come, on a rainy morning at 8:10 AM 16.06.2013, Sunday. I was born dark, not a color, liked by many in the world. But, my mom was the happiest person in the world to see me. My dad started calling all his relatives and friends to see me in the hospital. And guess what! There were so many people to see me that the security guard had to drive them away from the hospital.

Other than my parents, my grandparents were also one of the proudest members of the family. They took care of me like a princess. Even now, my grandparents take care of me. My grandmother is a great cook. She makes the best cupcakes, pizzas, donuts, cakes, etc. My mother can never cook like her, I'm sure. My grandfather is very smart, funny and strong. He gives me a lot of smart advises and keeps me humorous.

My first day of school was funny. My teachers and my friends thought I landed from the land of Africa. Little did they know, that my beautiful curly hair and my brown skin was a gift from my parents and a perfect plan by God. One of my cousin brother's little finger got stuck in my curly hair. And it took quite a while for my father to take out his finger out of my hair.

Now that feeling is hard to describe. Was I feeling happy, sad or shocked? I don't know haha. All I know it was a big relief once that little finger was out of my hair. How did his finger get in there? Was he on a treasure hunt? SERIOUSLY?? That was absurd.

Moving on...

My hair is thick, black and curly. I don't remember a day when I got my hair combed. My mother says, its high maintenance. It needs special shampoo, hair oil and conditioners. From shampoos to conditioners to serums, the curly hair routine is an exhausting and a tiring one. My relatives told my parents to shave off my hair as per the hindu customs but, my parents refused and my dad said to the rest of the relatives that he will never make me bald and the best part of me was my black curly hair. Indians are weird. Especially the ones who belong to the conservative families. For them, the definition of beautiful hair is long, straight, silky hair.

Then 1 year later, I shifted somewhere else. Also, Mumbai, but in the west. So, I went into another school. Ugh, online classes made me mad. Due to covid it was online. Anyways, that time I was in class 2A and I wasn't so much into studies like before, even in class 3A. I still studied. I shifted to a small place called Rajarhat (Located in West Bengal, Kolkata). Things went well, I was into studies again. I joined late. I made a lot of friends. Everyone was so obsessed with my hair. They ALWAYS asked the same stupid question: Are you from Africa?

My answer: NO, I just look like an African.

I can't believe everyone keeps asking me this. Only Unatee Prasad (one of my classmates) understands that I look like an Indian (Which I am). Everyone who thinks I am African, are the stupidest people on earth. OH WAIT! They never had a brain! I also sometimes feel like I'm getting used to this. During my exams, I started to take a break from my laptop and TV. I did well in the exams. I will do better in my final exam. I pray to Jesus that I will pass.

Virat is the naughtiest boy in my class. His full name is Virat Sharma. He dropped my bag, broke my compass box, told me I'm African and forced me to show my paper. When I told teacher about this, she scolded him and changed our places. I from now on sat with Ashmita (One of my classmates). Her full name is Ashmita Patra. She is friends with Pinki Pandit, Snigidha Karmakar and Medha Mishra (Also one of my classmates). They are my friends too.

We talked about the picnic to Eco park, but Ashmita planned for us to go to Aircraft Museum on the 24ᵗʰ of September because she had to go to visit her grandfather. We always talk about studies. We send notes to each other on what is going to come for the exams. I had made an Independence Day drawing. It was hung on the wall like everyone else's drawing. She gave me a new pen but everyone else's pen given to them by teacher was given earlier because I was absent.

I loved my pen a lot and I use it all the time. It is my favorite pen. She also took me downstairs while I didn't get my card yet. I would like to give a special thanks to Poulami Banerjee miss (my computer/class teacher).

** The End **

You Are Beautiful The Way You Are

Other good people deserve to have a life like me. I'm not saying that some of ya'll have to look like me, but however ya'll look, you are beautiful the way you are. Teenage era coming soon.